this book belongs to:

- -

- -

AIR MAIL

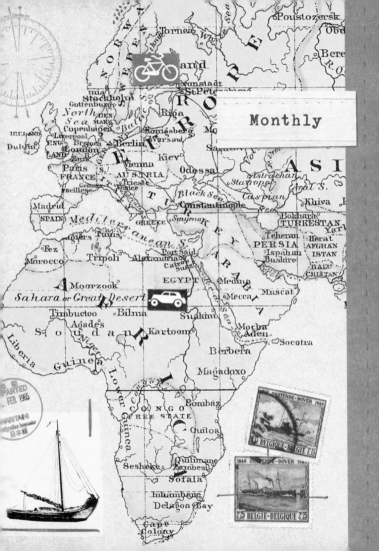

Monthly

Notes	Monday	Tuesday	Wednesd

Thursday	Friday	Saturday	Sunday

1 2 3 4 5 6 7 8 9 10 11 12

Notes	Monday	Tuesday	Wednesday

1 2 3 4 5 6 7 8 9 10 11 12

Thursday	Friday	Saturday	Sunday

Notes	Monday	Tuesday	Wednesday

Thursday	Friday	Saturday	Sunday

Notes	Monday	Tuesday	Wednesday

POST OFFICE
EXPRESS
DELIVERY

1 2 3 4 5 6 7 8 9 10 11 12			
Thursday	Friday	Saturday	Sunday

Notes	Monday	Tuesday	Wednesday

COMPROBANTE DE
PAGO POR ESTACION
DE PEAJE

Thursday	Friday	Saturday	Sunday

Notes	Monday	Tuesday	Wednesday

Thursday	Friday	Saturday	Sunday

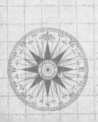

No one realizes how beautiful it is to travel
until he comes home and rests his head on his
old, familiar pillow.
— Lin Yutang

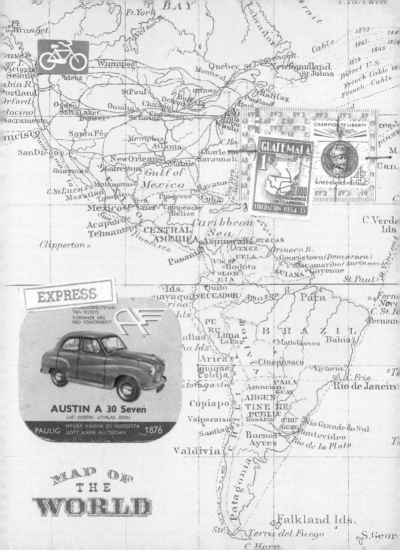

Notes	Monday	Tuesday	Wednesday

PAR AVION

1 2 3 4 5 6 7 8 9 10 11 12

Thursday	Friday	Saturday	Sunday

北京地下铁道车票

b 463 按销凭证   叁元 032843

Notes	Monday	Tuesday	Wednesday

PER VLIEGTUIG
PAR AVION

1   2   3   4   5   6   7   8   9   10   11   12

Thursday	Friday	Saturday	Sunday

Notes	Monday	Tuesday	Wednesday

日本郵便
NIPPON
★260
原宿駅前
HARAJUKU
EKIMAE
通用当日
★144053
28・02

Thursday	Friday	Saturday	Sunday

Notes	Monday	Tuesday	Wednesday

	1 2 3 4 5 6 7 8 9 10 11 12		
Thursday	Friday	Saturday	Sunday

Notes	Monday	Tuesday	Wednesday

Thursday	Friday	Saturday	Sunday

Notes	Monday	Tuesday	Wednesday

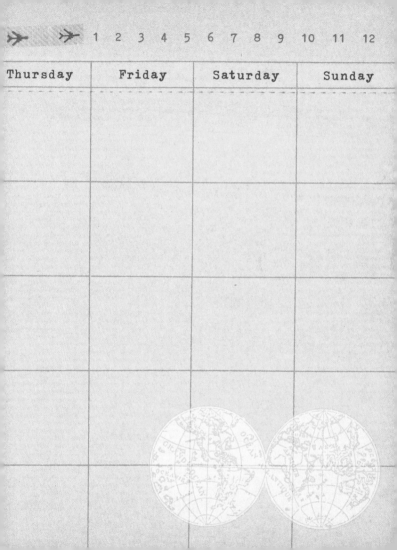

Thursday	Friday	Saturday	Sunday

Notes	Monday	Tuesday	Wednesday

ROYAL DUTCH
AIRLINES
SERVING 39 COUNTRIES THROUGHOUT THE WORLD
KLM

Thursday	Friday	Saturday	Sunday

Checklist

- [ ]
- [ ]
- [ ]
- [ ]
- [ ]
- [ ]
- [ ]
- [ ]
- [ ]
- [ ]
- [ ]
- [ ]
- [ ]
- [ ]

Checklist

Checklist

- [ ]
- [ ]
- [ ]
- [ ]
- [ ]
- [ ]
- [ ]
- [ ]
- [ ]
- [ ]
- [ ]
- [ ]
- [ ]
- [ ]

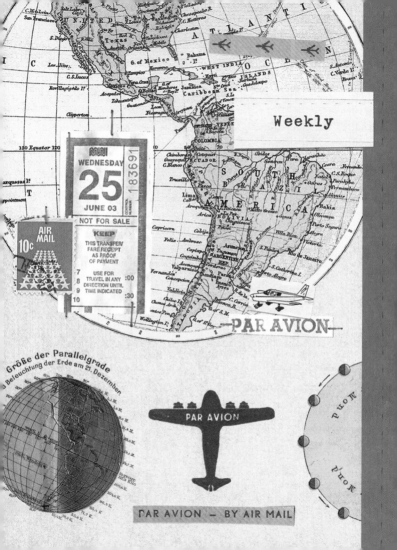

Weekly

MINI
WEDNESDAY
25
JUNE 03

183691

AIR MAIL 10c

NOT FOR SALE

KEEP
THIS TRANSFER/
FARE RECEIPT
AS PROOF
OF PAYMENT

USE FOR
TRAVEL IN ANY
DIRECTION UNTIL
TIME INDICATED

7   :00
8
9
10   :30

PAR AVION

Größe der Parallelgrade
a Beleuchtung der Erde am 21. Dezember

PAR AVION

PAR AVION — BY AIR MAIL

Weekly Plan

AIR MAIL
PAR AVION

Mon

Tue

Wed

Thu

Fri

Sat

Sun

| | JAN ○ | FEB ○ | MAR ○ | APR ○ | MAY ○ | JUN ○ |
| | JUL ○ | AUG ○ | SEP ○ | OCT ○ | NOV ○ | DEC ○ |

Mon

Tue

Wed

Thu

Fri

Sat

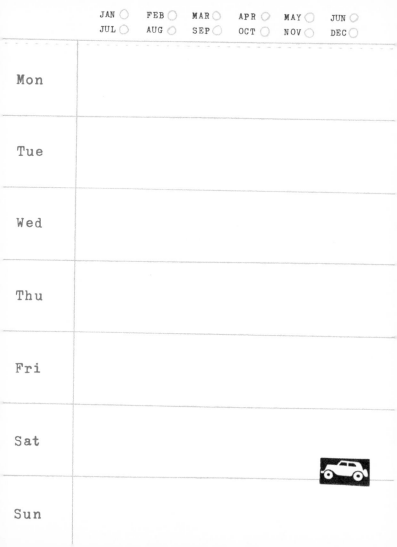

Sun

Weekly Plan

Mon	
Tue	
Wed	
Thu	
Fri	
Sat	
Sun	

JAN ◯   FEB ◯   MAR ◯   APR ◯   MAY ◯   JUN ◯
JUL ◯   AUG ◯   SEP ◯   OCT ◯   NOV ◯   DEC ◯

Mon

Tue

Wed

Thu

Fri

Sat

Sun

Weekly Plan

Mon	
Tue	
Wed	
Thu	
Fri	
Sat	
Sun	

| | JAN ○   FEB ○   MAR ○   APR ○   MAY ○   JUN ○ |
| | JUL ○   AUG ○   SEP ○   OCT ○   NOV ○   DEC ○ |

Mon	
Tue	
Wed	
Thu	
Fri	
Sat	
Sun	

Weekly Plan

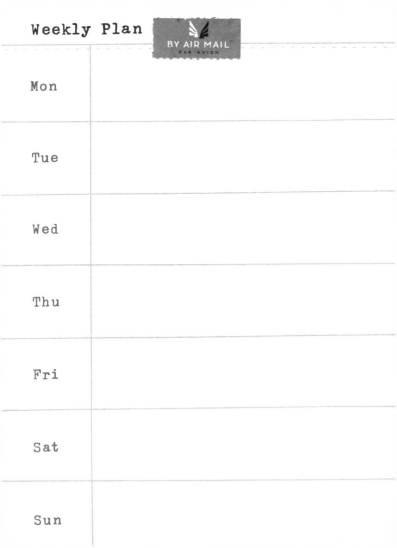

BY AIR MAIL
PAR AVION

Mon

Tue

Wed

Thu

Fri

Sat

Sun

| | JAN ○ | FEB ○ | MAR ○ | APR ○ | MAY ○ | JUN ○ |
| | JUL ○ | AUG ○ | SEP ○ | OCT ○ | NOV ○ | DEC ○ |

Mon

Tue

Wed

Thu

Fri

Sat

Sun

The world is a book and those who do
not travel read only one page.

— St. Augustine

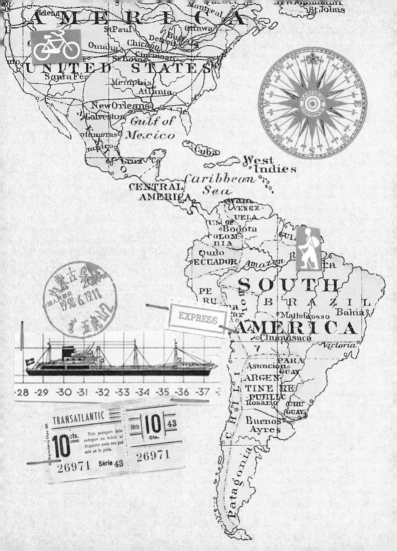

Weekly Plan

Mon

Tue

Wed

Thu

Fri

Sat

Sun

| JAN ○ | FEB ○ | MAR ○ | APR ○ | MAY ○ | JUN ○ |
| JUL ○ | AUG ○ | SEP ○ | OCT ○ | NOV ○ | DEC ○ |

Mon

Tue

Wed

Thu

Fri

Sat

Sun

Weekly Plan

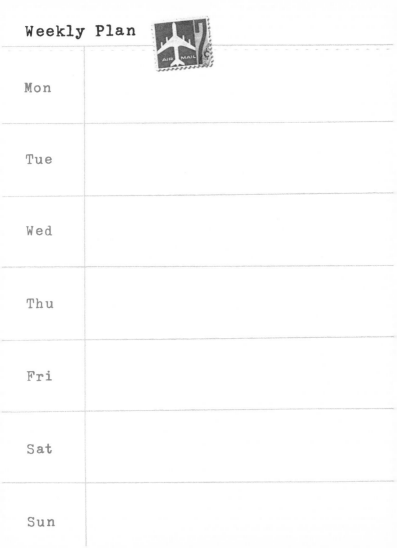

Mon	
Tue	
Wed	
Thu	
Fri	
Sat	
Sun	

JAN ○ FEB ○ MAR ○ APR ○ MAY ○ JUN ○
JUL ○ AUG ○ SEP ○ OCT ○ NOV ○ DEC ○

Mon

Tue

Wed

Thu

Fri

Sat

Sun

Weekly Plan

Mon	
Tue	
Wed	
Thu	
Fri	
Sat	
Sun	

| | JAN ○ | FEB ○ | MAR ○ | APR ○ | MAY ○ | JUN ○ |
| | JUL ○ | AUG ○ | SEP ○ | OCT ○ | NOV ○ | DEC ○ |

Mon

Tue

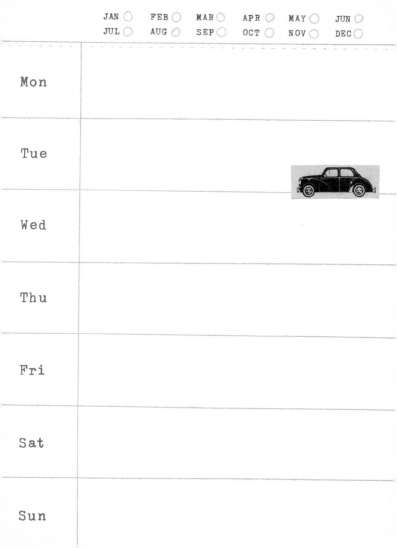

Wed

Thu

Fri

Sat

Sun

Weekly Plan

Mon

Tue

Wed

Thu

Fri

Sat

Sun

| | JAN ○ | FEB ○ | MAR ○ | APR ○ | MAY ○ | JUN ○ |
| | JUL ○ | AUG ○ | SEP ○ | OCT ○ | NOV ○ | DEC ○ |

Mon

Tue

Wed

Thu

Fri

Sat

Sun

BOARDING CARD

Our battered suitcases were piled on the sidewalk again; we had longer
ways to go. But no matter, the road is life.

— Jack Kerouac

Weekly Plan

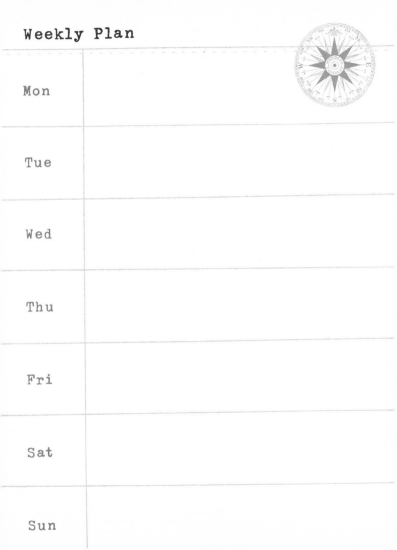

Mon	
Tue	
Wed	
Thu	
Fri	
Sat	
Sun	

Mon

Tue

Wed

Thu

Fri

Sat

Sun

Weekly Plan

Mon	
Tue	
Wed	
Thu	
Fri	
Sat	
Sun	

EXPRESS

-28 -29 -30 -31 -32 -33 -34 -35 -36 -37

JAN ◯   FEB ◯   MAR ◯   APR ◯   MAY ◯   JUN ◯
JUL ◯   AUG ◯   SEP ◯   OCT ◯   NOV ◯   DEC ◯

Mon

Tue

Wed

Thu

Fri

Sat

Sun

Weekly Plan

Mon	
Tue	
Wed	
Thu	
Fri	
Sat	
Sun	

| | JAN ○ FEB ○ MAR ○ APR ○ MAY ○ JUN ○ |
| | JUL ○ AUG ○ SEP ○ OCT ○ NOV ○ DEC ○ |

Mon

Tue

Wed

Thu

Fri

Sat

Sun

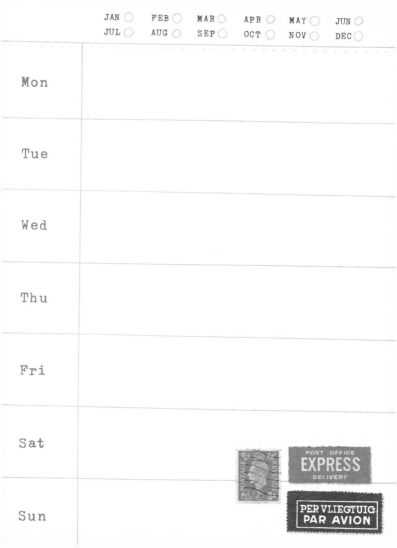

Weekly Plan

Mon

Tue

Wed

Thu

Fri

Sat

Sun

| | JAN ○ | FEB ○ | MAR ○ | APR ○ | MAY ○ | JUN ○ |
| | JUL ○ | AUG ○ | SEP ○ | OCT ○ | NOV ○ | DEC ○ |

Mon

Tue

Wed

Thu

Fri

Sat

Sun

It is better to travel than to arrive.

— Proverb

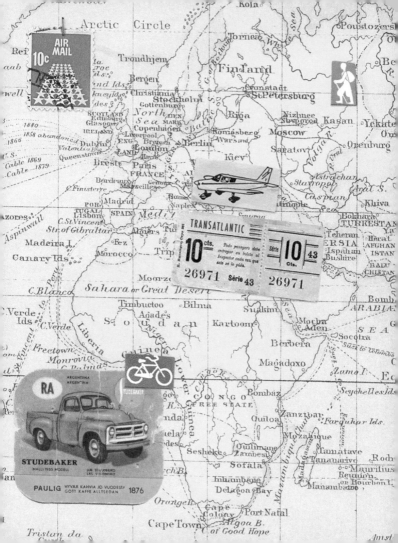

Weekly Plan

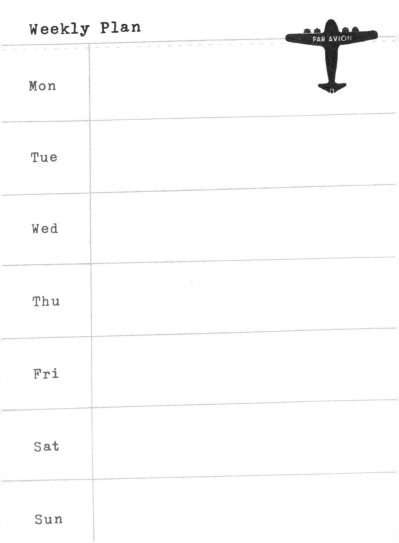

PAR AVION

Mon

Tue

Wed

Thu

Fri

Sat

Sun

| | JAN ○ | FEB ○ | MAR ○ | APR ○ | MAY ○ | JUN ○ |
| | JUL ○ | AUG ○ | SEP ○ | OCT ○ | NOV ○ | DEC ○ |

Mon

Tue

Wed

Thu

Fri

Sat

Sun

Weekly Plan

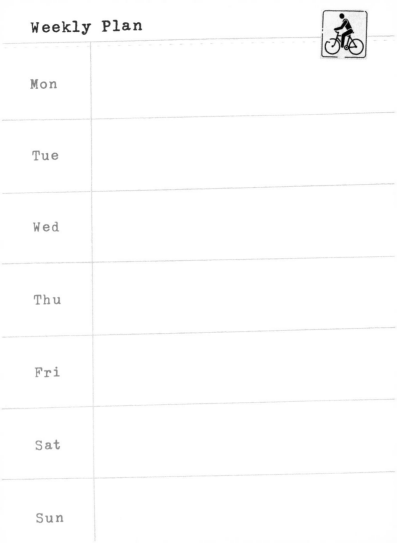

Mon

Tue

Wed

Thu

Fri

Sat

Sun

Mon

Tue

Wed

Thu

Fri

日本郵便
NIPPON
★260
原宿駅前
HARAJUKU
EKIMAE
適用当日限り
★14★
28・02・02

Sat

14053

Sun

Weekly Plan

Mon	
Tue	
Wed	
Thu	
Fri	
Sat	
Sun	

M — No. 55.

EXPRESS

PASSENGER TICKET

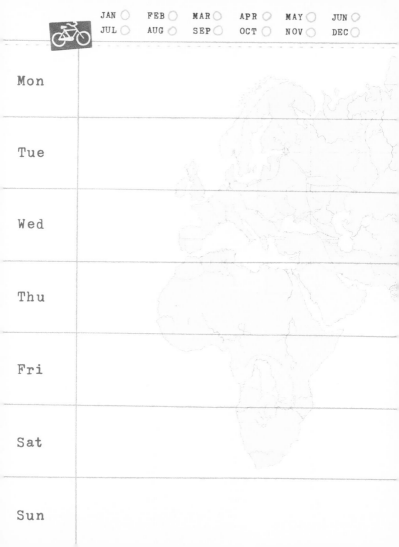

JAN ○   FEB ○   MAR ○   APR ○   MAY ○   JUN ○

JUL ○   AUG ○   SEP ○   OCT ○   NOV ○   DEC ○

Mon

Tue

Wed

Thu

Fri

Sat

Sun

Weekly Plan

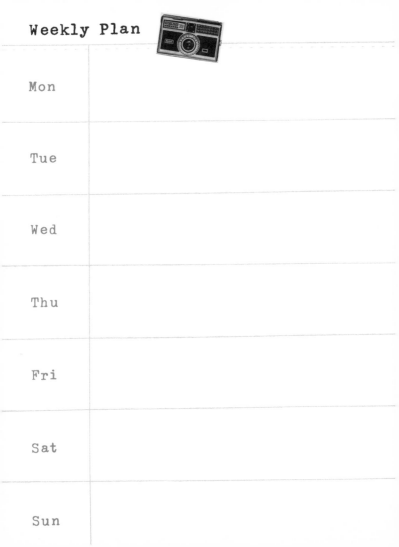

Mon

Tue

Wed

Thu

Fri

Sat

Sun

JAN ◯ FEB ◯ MAR ◯ APR ◯ MAY ◯ JUN ◯
JUL ◯ AUG ◯ SEP ◯ OCT ◯ NOV ◯ DEC ◯

Mon

Tue

Wed

Thu

Fri

Sat

Sun

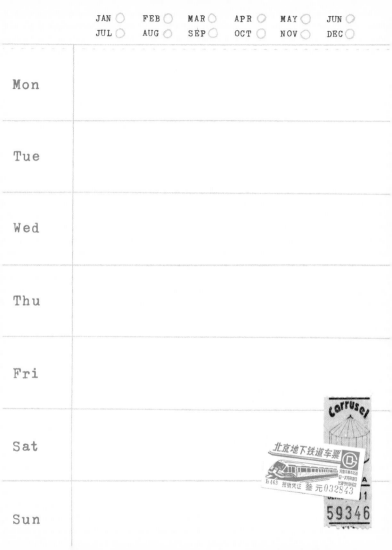

So throw off the bowlines, sail away from the
safe harbor. Catch the trade winds in your sails.
Explore. Dream. Discover.
— Mark Twain

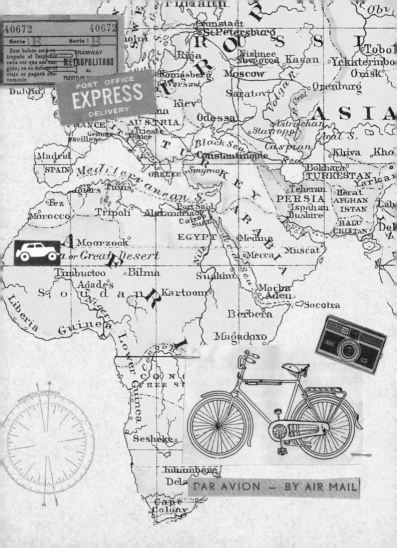

Weekly Plan

Mon	
Tue	
Wed	
Thu	
Fri	
Sat	
Sun	

JAN ○   FEB ○   MAR ○   APR ○   MAY ○   JUN ○
JUL ○   AUG ○   SEP ○   OCT ○   NOV ○   DEC ○

Mon

Tue

Wed

Thu

Fri

Sat

Sun

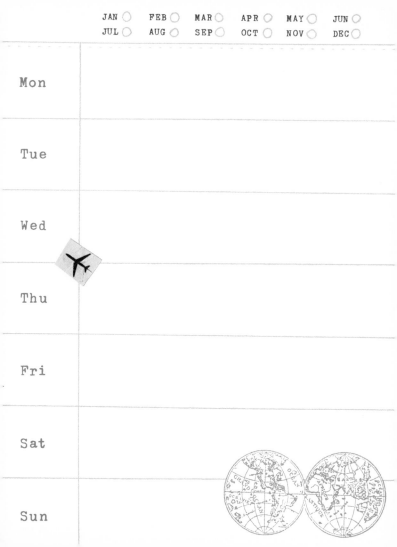

Weekly Plan

Mon	
Tue	
Wed	
Thu	
Fri	
Sat	
Sun	

	JAN ○	FEB ○	MAR ○	APR ○	MAY ○	JUN ○
	JUL ○	AUG ○	SEP ○	OCT ○	NOV ○	DEC ○

Mon

Tue

Wed

Thu

Fri

Sat

Sun

Weekly Plan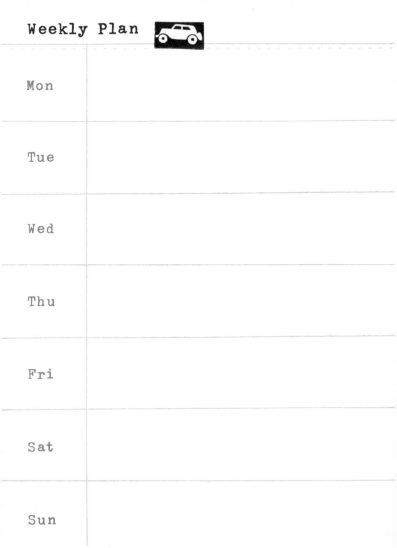

Mon

Tue

Wed

Thu

Fri

Sat

Sun

| | JAN ○ | FEB ○ | MAR ○ | APR ○ | MAY ○ | JUN ○ |
| | JUL ○ | AUG ○ | SEP ○ | OCT ○ | NOV ○ | DEC ○ |

Mon

Tue

Wed

Thu

Fri

Sat

Sun

Weekly Plan

Mon	
Tue	
Wed	
Thu	
Fri	
Sat	
Sun	

JAN ◯ FEB ◯ MAR ◯ APR ◯ MAY ◯ JUN ◯
JUL ◯ AUG ◯ SEP ◯ OCT ◯ NOV ◯ DEC ◯

Mon

Tue

Wed

Thu

Fri

Sat

Sun

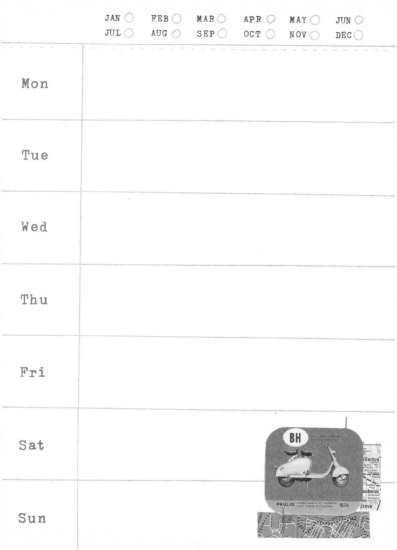

Blessed are the curious for they
shall have adventures.

— Lovelle Drachman

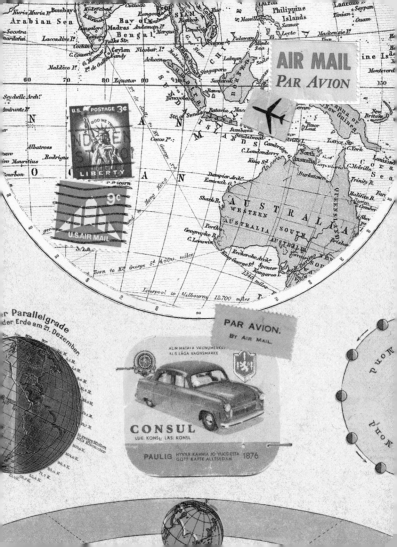

Weekly Plan

Mon	
Tue	
Wed	
Thu	
Fri	
Sat	
Sun	

BY AIR MAIL
PAR AVION

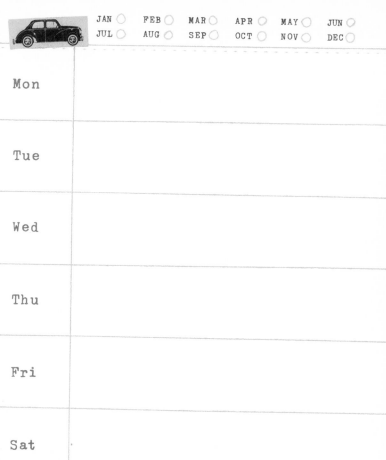

JAN ◯ FEB ◯ MAR ◯ APR ◯ MAY ◯ JUN ◯
JUL ◯ AUG ◯ SEP ◯ OCT ◯ NOV ◯ DEC ◯

Mon

Tue

Wed

Thu

Fri

Sat

Sun

Weekly Plan

Mon

Tue

Wed

Thu

Fri

Sat

Sun

JAN ◯   FEB ◯   MAR ◯   APR ◯   MAY ◯   JUN ◯
JUL ◯   AUG ◯   SEP ◯   OCT ◯   NOV ◯   DEC ◯

Mon

Tue

Wed

Thu

Fri

Sat

Sun

Weekly Plan

Mon

Tue

Wed

Thu

Fri

Sat

Sun

Mon

Tue

Wed

Thu

Fri

Sat

Sun

R No 3296²

Weekly Plan

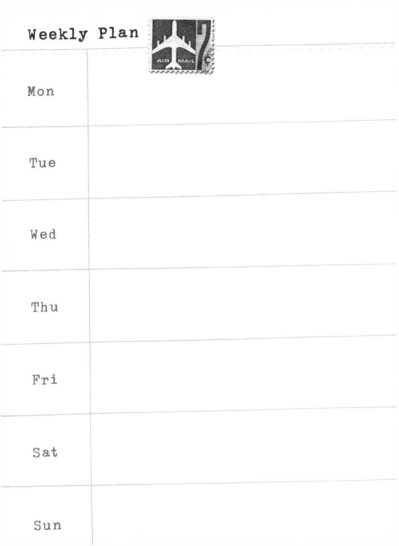

Mon	
Tue	
Wed	
Thu	
Fri	
Sat	
Sun	

| | JAN ○ | FEB ○ | MAR ○ | APR ○ | MAY ○ | JUN ○ |
| | JUL ○ | AUG ○ | SEP ○ | OCT ○ | NOV ○ | DEC ○ |

Mon

Tue

Wed

Thu

Fri

Sat

Sun

EXPRESS

FÖRSÄKER VÄG
MED KÖRKOMPART

AUSTIN A 30 Seven
LUE DÖÖTIN UTTALAS ÅSTN

PAULIG NYYLÄ KAHYIA VO HUODETTA
GOTT KAFFE ALLTSEDAN 1876

As you walk and eat and travel, be where you are, otherwise you will miss most of your life.

— Buddha

PER VLIEGTUIG
PAR AVION

PAULIG HYVÄÄ KAHVIA JO VUODESTA 1876
GOTT KAFFE ALLTSEDAN

Weekly Plan

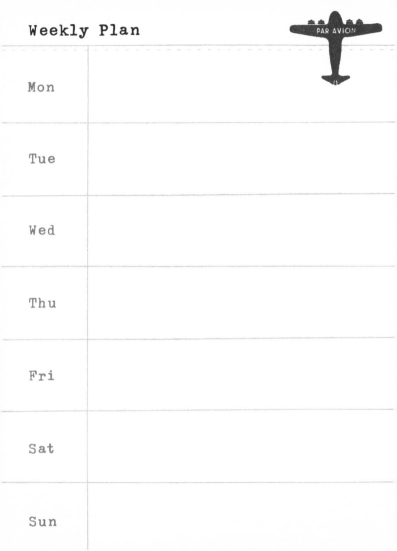

Mon	
Tue	
Wed	
Thu	
Fri	
Sat	
Sun	

JAN ◯   FEB ◯   MAR ◯   APR ◯   MAY ◯   JUN ◯
JUL ◯   AUG ◯   SEP ◯   OCT ◯   NOV ◯   DEC ◯

Mon

Tue

Wed

Thu

Fri

Sat

Sun

Weekly Plan

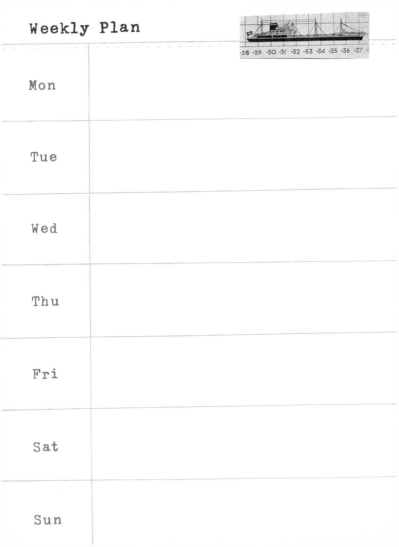

Mon

Tue

Wed

Thu

Fri

Sat

Sun

	JAN ○	FEB ○	MAR ○	APR ○	MAY ○	JUN ○
	JUL ○	AUG ○	SEP ○	OCT ○	NOV ○	DEC ○

Mon

Tue

Wed

Thu

Fri

Sat

Sun

Weekly Plan

Mon

Tue

Wed

Thu

Fri

Sat

Sun

Mon

Tue

Wed

Thu

Fri

Sat

Sun

Weekly Plan

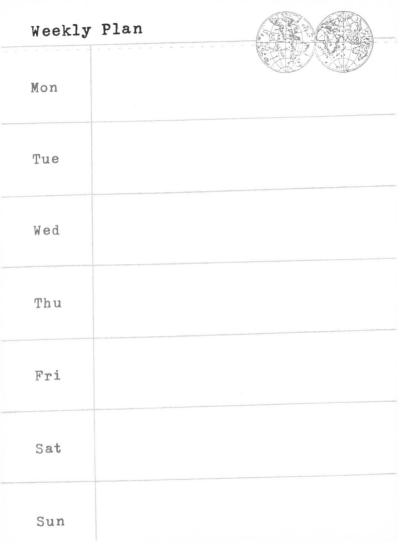

Mon

Tue

Wed

Thu

Fri

Sat

Sun

JAN ○ FEB ○ MAR ○ APR ○ MAY ○ JUN ○
JUL ○ AUG ○ SEP ○ OCT ○ NOV ○ DEC ○

Mon

Tue

Wed

Thu

Fri

Sat

Sun

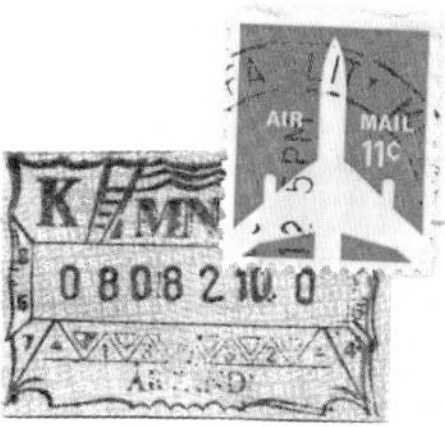

The first step in the journey is to lose your way.
— Galway Kinnell

Contacts

name   birthday

address

phone   e-mail

website

---

name   birthday

address

phone   e-mail

website

---

name   birthday

address

phone   e-mail

website

Contacts

name   birthday

address

phone   e-mail

website

---

name   birthday

address

phone   e-mail

website

---

name   birthday

address

phone   e-mail

website

Contacts

name   birthday

address

phone   e-mail

website

name   birthday

address

phone   e-mail

website

name   birthday

address

phone   e-mail

website

Contacts

name   birthday

address

phone   e-mail

website

name   birthday

address

phone   e-mail

website

name   birthday

address

phone   e-mail

website

Contacts

name   birthday

address

phone   e-mail

website

name   birthday

address

phone   e-mail

website

name   birthday

address

phone   e-mail

website

Contacts

name _____ birthday _____

address _____

_____

phone _____ e-mail _____

website _____

name _____ birthday _____

address _____

_____

phone _____ e-mail _____

website _____

name _____ birthday _____

address _____

_____

phone _____ e-mail _____

website _____

Contacts

name _____ birthday _____

address _____

_____

phone _____ e-mail _____

website _____

name _____ birthday _____

address _____

_____

phone _____ e-mail _____

website _____

name _____ birthday _____

address _____

_____

phone _____ e-mail _____

website _____

Contacts

name _____ birthday _____

address _____

_____

phone _____ e-mail _____

website _____

name _____ birthday _____

address _____

_____

phone _____ e-mail _____

website _____

name _____ birthday _____

address _____

_____

phone _____ e-mail _____

website _____

Contacts

name   birthday

address

phone   e-mail

website

name   birthday

address

phone   e-mail

website

name   birthday

address

phone   e-mail

website

40672 40672
Serie B Serie B
Este boleto será en
tregado al Inspector
cada vez que sea exi
gido; en su defecto el
viaje se pagará nue
vamente.

TRAMWAY
METROPOLITANO
AL
PUERTO 25 C

R Helsinki
Helsingfors
02376

Notes

北京地下铁道车票

b 463 投销凭证 叁 元 032843

DEPARTED
22. FEB. 1985
NARITA(N)
日本

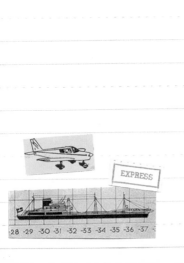

EXPRESS

-28 -29 -30 -31 -32 -33 -34 -35 -36 -37

MAGNETIC COMPASS

F.A. LINEA D. MITRE C/U.
RETIRO
V. LOPEZ
VALIDO PARA LA FECHA
Precio $ 0,32   Serie 00

The great difference between voyages rests not with
the ships, but with the people you meet on them.
— Amelia E. Barr

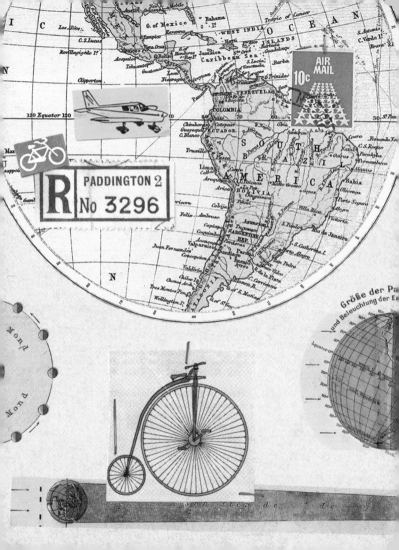

BOARDING CARD

AY 0667 K 27JAN1745

GATE	BOARD TIME	SEAT	SMOKE

ADDITIONAL SEAT   INFOR

POS   CK.WT.   UNCK. WT.   UNCK. WT.

BAGGAGE ID NR.

DOCUMENT NUMBER

2 105 9   ประเทศไทยTHAILAND   0